An Active Duty Entrepreneurs Guide To Purchasing Investment Properties

Real Estate Investing

Tyrone Dickens

The Labyrinth Of Scribblers Publishing LLC

Properties, Real Estate Investing

Disclaimer: This book and the information contained in this book are for general educational and information purposes only. Nothing contained in this book should be construed as or intended to guarantee a specific outcome. Users are encouraged to confirm the information contained herein with other sources and review the information carefully. The publisher and author shall not be liable for any direct, indirect, consequential, special, exemplary, or other damages arising from there.

For permission requests, or speaking engagements write the publisher at; Ty_Dickens@LabyrinthOfScribblers.com or;

The Labyrinth of Scribblers Publishing LLC
368 S. Pickett Street #22533
Alexandria, Virginia 22304-9996

Follow The Labyrinth Of Scribblers on Instagram
IG - @LabyrinthofScribblers
Follow the Labyrinth Of Scribblers on Facebook
Facebook/LabyrinthofScribblers
Follow The Labyrinth of Scribblers on Twitter
@LabyrinthofScribblers
www.youtube.com/MREI

LIBRARY OF CONGRESS CONTROL NUMBER
ISBN-13: 979-8-9851807-0-1 (eBook)
ISBN-13: 979-8-9851807-1-8 (Print)

Printed in the United States of America

Contents

Acknowledgments

Thank you, God! For every blessing disguised as a setback. For every lesson masked as a failed attempt, and all perceived losses returned many times over. I pray that you continue to cover me as I journey throughout this world. Through you, all things are possible.

Written and dedicated for the brave men and women of the United States Armed Forces who continually make the ultimate sacrifice while proudly serving the greatest nation in the world. I wholeheartedly thank you and your family for carrying the torch onward, protecting the liberties of citizens of this land and those around the world. Again, I humbly thank you.

I would like to thank my grandmother Dorothy for everything she has taught me. I rely on everything you've taught me, and I am forever grateful. Although I've failed time after time, I have never given up. You are a massive part of my success. May you rest in eternal peace. I love you. Tiger.

I would also like to thank my shipmate and friend of over twenty years SGT K. Stone, USMC. He motivated and encouraged me to share my wisdom with other service members, ensuring they would be knowledgeable about beginning the real estate investment process.

To Xalen Amari and Kaiden Alexander, thank you for motivating and inspiring me to be the absolute best example for you. You give me joy and direction. I am proud of you, and I love you more than you will ever know.

Last but certainly not least, I would like to thank my pillar of strength when I'm weary and motivator when I'm lazy. My beautiful slice of heaven on earth, Dr. A. L. Jeter, continually supports me and my many entrepreneurial business endeavors. Thank you for your love and patience.

To you, the purchaser, with your purchase, we will donate a portion of the proceeds to a Veteran's charity. I humbly thank you for your purchase, for with it, you and I together will be a blessing to others!

Preface

If you were to ask 100 different people about real estate investing, odds are you would receive 100 other answers. There is a myriad of paths to build your real estate investment portfolio – none are wrong, just different.

Believe it or not, despite the vast difference in salaries, some young Service Members are just like some young professional athletes. Often, they both come from families that lack wealth. At a very young age, they're both introduced to a new lifestyle and salary. Unfortunately, due to the lack of financial literacy, the mismanagement of money continues. A dollar is a dollar. Again, it's relative; however, if you can't manage $500, you can't manage $500,000. Financial literacy is the key to good money habits.

Thus, it sparks the ideals to further promote financial literacy and its importance more than ever to men and women of the Armed Forces. The fact that you've decided to learn about this topic places you in a unique position to change the trajectory of your family's financial future for generations to come. But, unfortunately, no one is coming to save you. Currently, 1.5 million Veterans between 18 and 35 live in poverty after exiting the military.

Increasing your financial literacy will give you a fighting chance to protect yourself and your family.

The word "easy" is subjective in all things, but especially in real estate, as we all have varying degrees of risk tolerance. Based on my experience, I have found the "buy and hold" method easier when obtaining property while on active duty. Yes, adversity will come to you no matter which path you choose. However, having sound fundamentals will place you in the best position to handle what may come your way. I wrote this book to educate and motivate young service members in the beginning stages of real estate investing. It can be done, and you CAN do it! After you've completed this book, please review part two, "The Active Duty Entrepreneurs Guide to Readying Your Home for a Tenant," for a further in-depth review. If you've done any research before selecting this book, you may be aware that there are a couple of ways to get into real estate investing. Methods such as House Flipping, House Hacking, Rehabbing, or the Buy, Rehab, Rent, Refinance, Repeat, also known as the "BRRRR" method, all offer unique ways and challenges. As a Service Member, your position will be two-fold; One, buying the home as a primary residence and two, later leasing the property upon your PCS to generate cash flow. Historically speaking, I have found that the buy and hold method has been the path of least resistance while enduring 9-month long deployments at sea and other U.S. military rigors while building financial freedom.

Introduction

If I can do it, guess what? So, can you! Many authors and motivators offer this phrase up so loosely, but many fail to deliver on the promise and can't fulfill their claims of filling in the missing pieces of the real estate investing puzzle. Specifically, the military's active duty service member component is often left out of the home buying real estate investing process altogether.

Three hundred twenty-nine million six hundred sixty-three thousand three hundred fifty citizens live in the U.S., and less than 1 percent of our population has served in the military. Less than 0.5 percent are currently serving as of today. Few will ever experience the honor of serving our great nation. Nor can they speak to our unique processes and nuances as military service members. These words are not an attack on our fellow citizens we swore an oath to protect, but insight as too often why we are left out or narrowly spoke of regarding real estate investing while serving our nation while on active duty. Which one can deduce to their lack of insight into how our various military branches operate. For situational awareness, ask at least five people, are they renting or investing in real estate? If you're lucky, you may get 1 out of 5 as an investor; if you were to ask why not, it would likely be due to a lack of targeted information.

With this book, feeling left out ends today! Armed with this book, you, as a member of the U.S. Armed Forces, will successfully increase your knowledge and navigate the seemingly complex real estate investing process from an active duty vantage point from Alpha to Zulu! That's A to Z for non-service members.

Granted, we're mature enough to know that not all situations are carbon copies. What may have worked for me may not work for the next. However, I will guide you through the core principles of the real estate investing process while on active duty. These core principles will ensure you receive factual information based on the federal law, my personal experience, sweat equity, and success achieved as an active duty real estate investor with over 2 million dollars in assets as an E6.

Within this book, you will also learn about credit's role and its importance to the home buying process. From down payments, and where to get money for your down payment such as; Thrift Savings Plan (TSP), the importance of, details of locating property, allocation of BAH, and much more!

Although this book is tailored primarily for the men and women within the Active Duty component of the U.S. Armed Forces; Retirees, Veterans, Spouses, Dependent Children, and Civilians alike will find this book extremely useful. For example, they will learn about the home loan benefits process from the U.S. Department of Veterans Affairs (DVA) as beneficiaries of VA home loan programs in the instance of the death of the sponsor/Service Member if applicable. Particularly, dependent spouses will learn to navigate VA homebuyer processes.

The 401k policy created in the eighties and used by large corporations saw the 20-year pension as a financial burden and offered additional savings to employers. As employees lived longer, so did the payout. Thus, the birth of the 401K. Under the new 401K, corporations passed the responsibility of the pension onto the hands of the employees. In short, you get out of it what you put into it.

The U.S. Military is, without a doubt, functioning like a fortune 500 corporation. Some branches earned recognition as "best places to work" in addition to excellent benefits. However, it too must trim the fat to ensure success for years to come. Should you retire, the Department of Veterans Affairs (DVA) budget will provide your future benefits. For FY2021, the DVA is requesting $243B, which is a 10.2 percent increase from the current FY2020 levels.

Since World War II, the U.S. military has offered an iteration of a 20-year retirement plan. Until recently, lawmakers mandated a change. As a result, recruits entering the military after 1 January 2018 will automatically be enrolled into the Blended Retirement System (BRS). Under the BRS, Service members will receive a retirement after 20 years, however, at a substantially reduced rate of a multiplier at 2 percent per year of service. In addition to what you opt to invest, the military will match up to 5 percent.

Simply put, the government created BRS to save money for the long term. Those adjustments currently allow the U.S. to retain $2B per year. Why is this important? Gone are the days of working 20 years and receiving a guaranteed monthly stipend that hedged decently, contingent on the area you reside against inflation. No one is coming to save you. Instead, we should utilize opportunities that leverage our guaranteed salaries and maximize the power to obtain alternate sources of investment income. The military, by salary alone, will never make you wealthy. However, what it does provide is the stability of a solid foundation to build. What will you build?

I will provide real-world scenarios based on my personal experience for each of the chapters. As a Service Member, your position will be two-fold. One, buying your home as a primary residence, and two, ultimately renting the property upon your

PCS to create a second stream of income. Investing in the right property may provide passive income with monthly cash flow and tax benefits.

You should not pursue the real estate investing process lightly as it is not a get-rich-quick scheme. Throughout this process, you should be brutally honest with yourself each step of the way to ascertain if real estate investing is for you. Wasting a professional's time, i.e., a realtor, home inspector, etc., throughout this process will burn bridges and may damage the possibility of a long-term business relationship. As time is money, and this is how they provide for their families in the industry.

The information within these pages supports the auspices of long-term investing. This information is essentially your "GQ drill" to save you time and stave off the potential loss of money. Do note, with any investment; there are risks and no guarantees throughout this process. You must execute your due diligence throughout the real estate investing process as the author, personnel mentioned within, or the publishing company assumes no responsibility for your actions, misfortunes, or fortunes. However, if executed properly, the decisions and sacrifices you make today may positively impact your family for generations to come.

My prayers are that this book will reach Soldiers, Sailors, Airmen, Marines, Coast Guardsmen, and Commissioned Officers very early in their careers and plant a seed of interest in real estate investing. I also pray for patience for the investor, as "the day you plant the seed is not the day you eat the fruit."

Let's get started!

Chapter One

Finding Your Why

Growing up, we didn't have a lot. I vividly recall the hole in my bedroom ceiling, which offered an unsolicited exposed view of the tree branches and the moon at night. The concrete center blockhouse was an old barn converted into a small house. The plywood flooring was splintered and deteriorating. White paint clippings that littered the ground around the house's exterior revealed its old age as it had worn down and peeled. Thin plastic lined the warped windows and served as a barricade to limit the draft on cold winter days. The house was in terrible shape. My sister and I wore old clothes and shoes. We didn't have video games or cable TV as it was a luxury item. In the absence of noticing what we didn't have, I did know that all we had were one another.

My mother did her best, but a young twenty-three-year-old single mother with two kids and zero help from our missing in action father could barely stay afloat financially. As you can imagine we moved a lot.

The school was supposed to be my haven, but it offered little solace. If my classmates weren't bullying me for not having name brands, some teachers would ridicule me. At times, I went several weeks without receiving a haircut. It wasn't a style, nor was I rebelling; it was a lack of resources. It was the late 80's, and I was only nine years old, and my teachers placed an insurmountable amount of responsibility and pressure on me for things beyond my control. Mr. Wilson made me cry as he openly insulted me on my appearance. I cried as I sat there at my desk. Somedays, we barely ate, so I was not thinking about my outward appearance.

I was miserable. Until one day, my grandmother visited my mother. My grandmother was a strong woman, and her daughters respected and feared her. My grandmother invited herself in and proceeded to give herself a tour of our little old center blockhouse, and she was not thrilled with what she had seen. I'll never forget her words or tone directed towards my mother. "You can do what you choose, but these children will not be living like this!" "Go get your things"! she shouted. My sister and I never moved so fast in our lives. I was throwing what little things I possessed in an old plastic Piggly Wiggly bag, as it would serve as our makeshift suitcase for the little belongings we did have. That was the last time I recall living with my mother.

My mother tried, but her efforts paled compared to what my grandmother could provide: stability. My grandmother was the established eldest of 14 children. She grew to be a disciplined, organized, and structured woman. During our time together, she taught me so much. At times, I was a mischievous child, and during my episodes of misbehaving, my punishments were to read from a very heavy old dictionary. I was relegated to following her around the house reading words to her at random. I can still smell that old brown thick dictionary. Considered abuse from a child's perspective was merely one of her many unorthodox ways of educating me.

My grandmother was a widow, as my grandfather died in a tragic car accident during the seventies. Left alone to raise six girls on her own, she knew she had to prepare. She was the first in her family to have a home built from the ground up in a very nice subdivision. Her home was constant and stable, as she provided shelter for so many in need over the years.

Saving, investing, and ownership was drilled into my head regularly over the years. Of all things discussed next to education, becoming a homeowner was at the top of her list. As she stressed and shared the importance of homeownership, the "how" was missing from her teachings.

Although my grandmother is no longer with us, her home still stands as strong as she did, and it is still in our family to this day. Whenever I visit my old neighborhood, I drive by what I consider my childhood home as it is currently being rented and provides a stream of income. It brings me joy to see the children running and playing as I once did. Her home serves as a reminder for me, and it reinforces one of her coined expressions; "If I can achieve and amass the things that I have with a sixth-grade education, then you should be able to do twice as much, now go!"

Indeed, I did; I joined the U.S. Navy at the age of 17. Abandoning all things familiar in exchange for dress blues and being haze gray and underway. Sent off into the world, armed with the foundational teachings from my grandmother – I was ready, or so I thought. I knew I had to become a homeowner, and I had to do it in a way to make my grandmother proud. My desire to make her proud fueled my passion for real estate investing.

Like countless others lacking good financial literacy, I, too, was unaware of the many things that had a significant role and impacted the entire home buying process before starting my journey. For example, negotiating, knowing the difference between the various mortgage loans; Conventional, Jumbo, or ARMs, etc., all topped with the perplexity of the military, created some additional hurdles as well.

If you're wondering what happened to the old center block barn house, it is no longer standing. Although it did last several years after joining the military, I would visit and reflect on my life and where I came from. Before the demolition, I would drive by that old house that gave me nightmares. It, too, served as motivation for me. I will always work hard and make the best long-term decisions and sacrifices to avoid ever living like that again. I will always speak of that house, for it plays a significant role in who I am today, a successful retired Navy Veteran and Real Estate Investor turned author.

Albeit my childhood may not have been picture perfect in the eyes of others, I wouldn't change one thing about my upbringing. We have stories that have shaped or molded us in some fashion, but your past doesn't have to define your future. Your future is yours to mold, and you can be whatever you choose to be!

Chapter Two

Understanding Your LES & BAH

By now, you should already be familiar with the Leave and Earning Statement (LES). However, since I don't know where you are within the stage of your career you are in, I will briefly cover the LES as it is ground central for your financial information and marries the real estate investing program together.

If you have already served at least ten years or more, you've probably uttered the phrase "I wish I would have had this information when I first enlisted!" at least once by now. I sure have, and I know a lot of others have too. My goal is to spark an interest and aid in a service member's foundation for long-term goals and objectives for real estate. If you are senior in rank, bear with us to ensure our junior shipmates are not educationally left behind, as we cover a couple of things you may already know.

The LES provides an in-depth review of monthly pay and allowances and other entitlements. It is issued monthly and accessed via the Defense Finance Accounting Service (DFAS) website www.dfas.mil. The LES contains seventy-eight fields of data. Although all fields are essential, we will focus on field 10, known as entitlements. Within field 10, you will find your Base pay, special or incentive pay, and allowances like Basic Allowance for Housing (BAH) or Subsistence (BAS). Field 11 is known as the Deductions Field, home to monthly Thrift Savings Plan (TSP) contributions, taxes, and other withholdings, which withholdings will be covered later in the book.

BAH is a stipend granted to subsidize living expenses and varies by geographical location, pay grade, and dependency status. BAH is provided in addition to your salary and is not a taxable source of income. For a complete list of BAH rates, visit BAH Calculator. You should consider BAH when factoring in your future duty stations to prevent economic hardships and maximize leveraging BAH to its full potential. For some locations such as San Francisco, California. Command Financial Screenings are a requirement due to their expensive nature. San Francisco boasts the highest BAH rate in the country as an E1 may receive $4,311.

I consider San Diego a sweet spot for real estate investing. Due to its climate, housing demand, and relative affordability compared to its northern neighbor San Francisco. For instance, BAH rates for various locations for Calendar year 2021 for military personnel are shown below and are as follows;

Enlisted BAH Rates for San Diego, California Zip Code 91942

- An E4 With Dependents: $2,691.00
- An E4 Without Dependents: $2,019.00
- An E5 With Dependents: $2,949.00
- An E5 Without Dependents: $2,268.00
- An E6 with dependents: $3,192.00
- An E6 without dependents: $2,460.00

Enlisted BAH Rates for Jacksonville, Florida Zip Code 32201

- An E4 With Dependents: $1,617.00
- An E4 Without Dependents: $1,320.00
- An E5 With Dependents: $1,674.00
- An E5 Without Dependents: $1,470.00
- An E6 with dependents: $1,809.00

•An E6 without dependents: $1,557.00
Enlisted BAH Rates for Norfolk, Virginia Zip Code 23510
•An E4 With Dependents: $1,734.00
•An E4 Without Dependents: $1,365.00
•An E5 With Dependents: $1,737.00
•An E5 Without Dependents: $1,602.00
•An E6 with dependents: $1,887.00
•An E6 without dependents: $1,731.00

Typically, BAH rates increase by 2.8 to 3.7 percent on 1 January of each calendar year. However, the data will change yearly; consult the referenced source of BAH rates for accuracy.

Each branch of service authorizes BAH entitlements by pay-grades differently. Therefore, additional administrative actions may be required for single service members without dependents to obtain BAH. The Commanding Officer may grant authorization to receive with dependent BAH only after providing proof of your dependents. Consult with your admin or finance office for the most up-to-date guidance on local command policy.

If you are in the early stages of your career and have minimal financial obligations, negative equity assets, or debts, it is possible to survive on your Base Pay alone. It will be tight, but you can do it with your sacrifice. A challenging yet straightforward rule to follow is, if it doesn't make you money, don't buy it. As living on your base pay alone will allow more income towards your mortgage and savings. Remember, by keeping your "overhead" low; you can allocate more funds from your discretionary income to the mortgage if you do not increase your debt-to-income ratio.

Properly utilizing your BAH early in your career is your best chance as it is a potent financial tool. Would you voluntarily write a check for the sum of $2,000 monthly, not as an investment but never to be seen again? Odds are, probably not. Living in base housing or renting an apartment on the economy each month is the equivalent of giving away your hard-earned money to a stranger with nothing in return. We can agree that you must find lodging; however, shouldn't that lodging be a property you own that accrues equity all while being paid for while you're on active duty by you and future tenants?

Most tour rotation lengths are on average three to five years. An investor could use the amount of equity gained over that period in the future for significant repairs, a down payment on your next property, or college tuition, etc.

Investing in Real Estate while in the military is very much so about strategy and will require research on local housing prices, rental markets on your part before selecting orders for your new duty assignments. Granted, the needs of the U.S. Military will come first. However, choosing an area with moderate housing prices increases the potential to maximize your BAH will help you a great deal. The goal is to find affordable housing in a location with a higher BAH.

"Be a Sharon..."

Fear, by definition, is an unpleasant feeling triggered by the perception of danger, real or imagined. A significant factor preventing service members from becoming homeowners while on Active Duty is fear of the unknown. "What will happen when I PCS from the area?" If you live in an apartment, I can assure you that it is implausible that the owner of your large apartment complex is your neighbor. I, too, succumbed to the fear attributed to analysis paralysis, which is reaching a point of analyzing potential outcomes and becoming paralyzed by the results yielded from my thoughts and not taking any action at all.

Fear drives uncertainty when derived from a lack of knowledge. During my first tour in Washington D.C. on the staff of Chief of Naval Personnel, I met a fellow Yeoman by the name of Sharon. Sharon was one of the sharpest working Sailors I have ever met. Eager, bold, and determined always to grab life by the horns and succeed. One morning while opening, she brought to my attention details of new housing development and planned to purchase a condo and felt I could benefit from buying property.

The National Harbor, which sits upon the land where a plantation once stood, is located south of Washington D.C. and rests adjacent to the Potomac River. After a fire destroyed the plantation house, the owner placed the land for sale. Although the slave quarters are viewable for historical purposes, the newly redeveloped land is home to condos, townhomes, hotels, shops, restaurants, and the MGM casino. Although Disney later pulled their plans to develop a resort, the news alone created hype and gave future value to the area.

The development occurred during the recession of 2008. Even during this era of a national mortgage crisis, my shipmate was determined to be a homeowner. Unfortunately, I was rendered crippled by my inaction – the ship had sailed, and I had missed the ship's movement. Sharon went on to purchase her two-bedroom condo with a mortgage of $1100. Stuck – I continued to lease my 800 square feet, one-bedroom for $1098 per month for two more years until I eventually PCS'ed. Sharon opted to house hack and leased her second bedroom to another Sailor for $750 per month until she PCS'ed a couple of years later, ultimately leading to the entire unit converting to a rental receiving $1,950 per month.

Sharon eventually sold the property sometime later, only to clear over $100K in profits. We all have our course to navigate, so I have no regrets about my actions or inactions, as those are her blessings. My lessons obtained during this era were strategizing and preparing myself for my next duty station so that I, too, can capitalize on future opportunities. Real estate is exciting, especially when you first start. Of course, you'll want to share with others as you learn more and see the benefit, but everyone won't see your vision. Yet, I urge you to continue on your course and not be discouraged. Instead, be bold, steadfast, and courageous - Be a Sharon.

Chapter Three

Military Privatized Base Housing

Upon arriving in San Diego, I initially stayed with a shipmate I'd been stationed with years prior in Naples, Italy. Larry had a massive home, and his family welcomed me. Living with Larry allowed me to take my time and not have the normal PCS pressures of rushing to obtain lodging and waste money on renting a space I wouldn't physically be in for months, as I would later fly to meet my ship already on deployment.

Months later, I returned with the USS JARRETT from deployment. With less than a three-year tour in front of me, it was time to find a place to call home. After experiencing the traffic horrors of Washington D.C. for four years, I knew I wouldn't be up for a long commute, so I settled in a luxury apartment located on Friars Road. The rent was $2,400 per month, and my BAH was only $2,184 per month. The first year alone, I paid $28,800 renting an apartment that I would never have any financial claim to the funds. Let's take a moment and allow that to sink in for a second. Twenty-eight thousand dollars is the average median income in my hometown. Better yet, it is the price of a fully-loaded midsize family sedan for perspective's sake. Yes, San Diego is relatively expensive, more so than the rural two-stoplight town from which I hail. I understand, but because you receive a lot doesn't mean you have to spend a lot – especially while renting. We, as Service Members, use a copout when we say "the government is paying for it" to justify our excessive spending. No. Those are your hard-earned funds, and we must learn to leverage our comparably small salaries and use our money as a tool. Personally, after seeing the numbers, I knew I had to make a change.

Seasick with the thought of having given so much money away, I immediately devised a plan. My strategy would require that I leave the luxury apartment and move into base housing while searching for a home to purchase. At the end of my lease, I moved to La Mesa military housing.

Just as the civilian sector has luxury apartments, the military does as well, but like all luxury items, they come at a cost, and you get what you pay for as the funds will derive from your BAH. Living in base housing in San Diego is a fantastic headache-free experience. Although the costlier higher-end base housing is adorned with beautiful uniformed tan stucco exteriors, with auburn colored rooftops, you'll pay no utilities for the use of central heating and cooling, accompanied by garage parking and maintenance. Point Loma, for example, is located often minutes from the base, the Exchange, Commissary, and gym. Those manicured lawns are beautiful but expensive over time, as after your three-year tour, you walk away with absolutely nothing. However, if you allow renting costly items to entice you for the moment, it will delay your process of homeownership for the future.

Although privatized Base Housing also takes a hefty chunk from your wallet, there are some advantages. One of the benefits of military housing is that it allows you the flexibility to break your lease with zero penalties to buy a home if you show your mortgage contract as proof of purchase. Living in military housing was an integral part of my plan, as breaking a lease and ruining my credit by renting on the civilian economy was not a viable strategic option. Therefore, I opted not to renew my lease at this beautiful apartment complex overlooking the mall on

Friars Road and move into less expensive and desirable base housing in La Mesa.

There are very few times when you may legally break a lease while renting on the civilian economy without being sued. Under the Service Members Civil Relief Act (SCRA), if you are PCSing or deploying for more than 90 days is one of the few times you may break your lease. Unfortunately, I wasn't doing either, so this wouldn't work for me. The SCRA protects Soldiers, Sailors, Airmen, Marines, Coast Guardsmen, and Commissioned Officers from being sued while in active military service of the United States for up to one year after military service. To be sure, before signing a lease of any type, inquire with your leasing office as to whether there is a clause protecting military service members from avoiding being held financially responsible.

Without the protection of the SCRA, which is an automatic entitlement for service members, if you decide to break your lease, most often, the fine print will hold you responsible for the remainder of rent owed, legal fees, etc. Additionally, they may go as far as damaging your credit.

During my earlier military days, Base Housing was operated and controlled by Department of the Navy (DoN) civilians that worked directly for the department. Nowadays, most base housing is "Privatized" and contracted out to Military Property Management & Development companies to save the Department of Defense (DoD) funding.

Currently, there are 36 military housing locations scattered across the San Diego area. The beautiful Village at NTC is trendy as it caters to E1 – E6 and is located 8 miles from Naval Station San Diego. This prestigious location is in high demand by young Service Members due to its premium location and amazing commute time. But, again, you're still "renting" and giving the government back your hard-earned money as the price could reach beyond $2,000 per month is unacceptable.

With all things in life, you get what you pay for, as the adage goes. By opting to move into the lackluster La Mesa base housing, the conveniences afforded to me were; utilities covered, security, and ample space, to name a few. However, the property I chose had seen better days, but the price was commensurate with the condition, location, etc. Again, I knew my move would require some sacrifices such as; longer commutes, residing in older homes, no garage, to name a few, and it was well worth it. The price I paid per month for living in La Mesa military housing was $1,450, which allowed me to save $734 per month after my move.

In conclusion, it's safe to say that your lodging is an essential requirement. However, whether you've opted for privatized military housing or choose to rent on the civilian economy, remember you don't have to choose the pricier option that you'll never own. Instead, implement a strategy that will allow you to pocket more of your money that will go toward the purchase of your future investment property and a condition to break your lease without penalties if necessary. Remember to keep your monthly expenses and overhead low!

"Stay Low..."

While stationed in Mayport, Florida, aboard USS THE SULLIVANS (DDG-68), I was the epitome of a young and carefree 17-year-old Sailor. My only expense was my Bell South mobile phone. I was traveling from country to country at the expense of the government while serving our country. Life was great! My only objective was to save as much money as I could. Unfortunately, this mentality wasn't mutual amongst some of my other shipmates.

The nineteen nineties birthed the era of twenty-inch chrome wheels, solidifying the benchmark of what a nice car should be. A fellow shipmate by the name of Fonzo had gotten himself caught up in the matrix. Imagine, if you will, a blue Ford Mustang with a white convertible top. All nicely coupled with white leather interior and tv's in the headrest. His trunk was complete with four ten-inch subwoofers, all while sitting on twenty-inch rims. For comparison's sake, this car was as desirable as the Dodge Charger or Challenger in the present day. Fonzo's car was amazing, I can't lie, but my logic would only allow me to see the negative equity. The car, the speakers, twenty-inch chrome wheels, two amps, tv's in the headrest were all financed at ridiculous interest rates.

Fonzo was in serious debt. My nature has continuously operated under the "win-win" philosophy. One evening while preparing to depart for liberty, Fonzo could be seen lounging around the berthing. I immediately thought it was odd, as we were in the same duty section and it wasn't like him to be on the ship on a non-duty day. A sulking Fonzo approached my rack, "what do you have planned for the night" he asked. The usual I replied, "hit the scene and see what I can get into." What about you? "Nothing, man... I'm broke... my car takes all of my money!" Thinking win-win, I made him an offer. "Look, how about you roll with me? I'll pay your way into the club, food after the club, fill your car up with gas and be your designated driver – so what do you think?" Fonzo's face lit up instantly. "Will you wait for me to get dressed? he laughed." Of course.

As I sat there waiting, the situation solidified my reasons for saving and living within my means. In 1996 as an E1, I earned $874 per month. After deductions, $748 at a bi-weekly rate of $374 per pay period after taxes. To say things were tight is an understatement. I did not purchase my first car until I reached my 5-year mark. I bought a 1994 Saturn SL2 with a salvaged title from a friend headed out on a WESTPAC. The heat and air conditioning did not work, which would have been fine, except living in Hawaii can get a little warm. The car was so hot my friends nicknamed it "The Furnace." It was a significant sacrifice and very much worth the hot days. I paid $2,500 for the car, and it lasted a very long time as the car not only survived Hawaii but my tour in Naples, Italy, and Washington D.C. Later, I donated the car to a family member.

For some, purchasing a car is driven by your emotions. Typically buying a new car generates a sentence containing five words that momentarily stroke your ego. For instance, "Man, that car looks good" or "Wow, that thang ready boy"! After the novelty or desire to hear those words wear off and time passes by, you'll realize it's just a car. Odds are, for some duty stations, you may require a car. If you find yourself in this position, before purchasing, remove your ego and opt for affordable, safe, and reliable. Fonzo's credit remained contained in a depreciating liability. Had he attempted to purchase a home at this time, he would have learned that his debt-to-income (DTI) may have been too high. Therefore, keep your overhead and monthly expenses low.

Chapter Four

Credit

For so many Americans, the dream of homeownership is further away primarily due to poor credit history. Your credit score is the gateway to your path of homeownership, as it will provide insight into the likeliness of you repaying the loan. Your score is also used as a qualifier and will also play a massive role in the interest rate you receive on your home loan. The difference between one percent could save or cost you tens of thousands of dollars throughout the mortgage loan.

Credit is the ability of a customer to obtain goods or services before payment, based on the trust that the borrower will make the payments at a later date. Credit is a factor in everything you do as an American. It is a factor for auto insurance, auto loans, home loans, credit cards, cellular phones, and much more. It even goes as far as impacting the life insurance premium you'll pay.

I know you're excited, and you should be! Before you do anything, and I mean anything. Obtain your credit report. Before you contact a realtor, before you shave or hug your spouse, I think you get the point that you should pull your credit report. The earlier, the better, as you could start rectifying any mishaps or FUBAR on your credit report.

Before the days of my willingness to use online bill pay, during my PCS move to San Diego Naval Special Warfare

Group THREE from the Pentagon, My previous command didn't forward my mail to me. Amid everything that comes with PCS'ing, I forgot to make a car payment, and it was late by thirty days, and the finance company did not spare a second, ensuring it was reflected on my credit report as late. Again, life happens! I found the error in time, and I disputed it with the "did not receive mail option," and the credit bureaus rectified my issue… or so I thought, we'll get into that in Chapter 9.

I'm sure you have an app on your smartphone which "monitors" your credit score. Unfortunately, "that's not it Chief", as it may not be as accurate as of the source. I've found that the numbers are off by sometimes more than 30 points! Therefore, it would behoove you to directly obtain your report from the exact agencies your lender will utilize; TransUnion, Experian, and Equifax. By federal law, under the Fair Credit Reporting Act, you may obtain six free copies of your credit report annually from Equifax or by calling 1-866-349-5191. In addition to one free annual report from www.AnnualCreditReport.com. Getting your credit report will arm you with your financial history in preparation for your mortgage loan application.

Credit scores consist of the following components; Payment history, the amount you owe, length of credit history, new credit, and the type of credit accounts. Credit scores ranges vary depending on the scoring model. Credit Scores range from 300 to 850. The most common score range places a score of 720 to 850 is considered excellent, 660-719 is considered good, 620 – 659 falls within the Fair/Limited range, and 300-619 is unfortunately Bad. A rate of 720 and above places you in an excellent position by placing you on course to receive the best possible interest rate.

Only 38 percent of Americans have excellent credit. Seventeen percent are within the Good category. Thirteen percent have Fair/Limited credit, and thirty-one percent fall into the bad credit category.

If your credit score is less than 720 but higher than 520, don't despair. Statistically speaking, you may still qualify for a mortgage loan. Granted, at potentially higher interest rates, but the approval odds are in your favor. On the other hand, if you possess a score of 520 or less, you may have some work to do before you're ready for homeownership with great rates.

Americans often don't check their credit until they are ready to make a significant purchase, but it may be too late by then. For instance, my cousin rarely reviewed his credit report. Then, one day he decided he wanted to purchase a new car. He pulled his credit report and found that someone had stolen his identity and he was a homeowner. His credit score was terrific! However, he never applied for a mortgage loan to purchase the home. After months of inquiries, someone erroneously added his social security number to another account. Even if you're not in the market, it is always a good idea to request your FREE credit report annually.

Requesting your credit annually from official sources won't lower your credit score. However, it would be wise not to obtain additional credit such as a revolving credit card to your favorite furniture store during the home buying process. Unnecessary credit inquiries will ultimately lower your score. Each hard credit inquiry decreases your credit score by three to five points each. In addition, the ten percent you save at check out for opening the card may cost you big bucks down the line, as this will impact your credit score and may affect your debt-to-income ratio and future interest rates. Those three to five points may seem small, but it seems almost impossible to increase your score after it has fallen. Debt-to-Income (DTI) ratio is a measurement of a borrower's ability to repay the loan. A high DTI is the number one reason mortgage applications are approved.

Possessing good credit is a requirement for military service. It also reflects on you, and if there are issues, you should work to rectify them to good standing. However, we're human, and life happens, so some may occasionally get off course. If you possess a Top-Secret Clearance Security Clearance (TS/SCI), do not attempt to hide it; immediately self-report or make it known during the periodic investigation. Failure to do so may jeopardize your career and limit your ability to serve. Seek help immediately, and with a plan, you'll be on the road to improving your credit score.

Tips for Improving Your Credit Score

As we've discussed, credit in good standing is essential. Remember, you didn't get into debt overnight, so that you won't get out of it overnight. Patience is a crucial contributor to repairing your credit standing. If applicable, here are some tips that could help you on your journey to credit improvement.

Devise a plan by instituting a budget and adhering to the confines you've set within your budget.

Pay your bills on time. Most financial institutions have some form of autopay and may offer you savings if you opt to use this feature. Paying your debt on time communicates to creditors that you are responsible.

Pay off debt and keep balances low on credit cards and other revolving debt. The industry standard of credit utilization is 30%. Instead, use 25% to ensure you don't cross the threshold, negatively impacting your credit due to usage.

Never arbitrarily close credit cards. A long credit history in good standing will work in your favor, as the length of credit is another key ingredient to strengthening it.

Avoid co-signing for family and friends. Their issues, good or bad, will impact your credit and may leave you responsible for the additional financial burden.

Open a secure credit card. A deposit in the amount of the credit received will be required. However, the deposit may be returned after a period of responsible credit use. The account may convert to a non-secured credit card. Pay on time and maintain low credit utilization.

Become an authorized user on the credit card account of a responsible cardholder of a family member, i.e., mother, father, or sibling, with excellent credit history. Having been added to someone else's card will require transparency by both parties as you will provide your SSN for addition to the account. During this period, open communication is the key, as you will likely want to know the account's status to remain in good standing. Ensure to destroy the physical card issued in your name.

Dispute any inaccuracies on your credit report immediately. It would be best if you disputed credit inquiries for longer than two years.

If you owe a debt, paying an additional amount per month before the end of the billing cycle will give your score a boost.

Chapter Five

Budget Forecast

Whether you are in excellent shape credit-wise or not, everyone should have a budget. Men lie, women lie, but the numbers don't.

To reiterate, information as mentioned earlier, this section also requires you to be completely honest with yourself. During this "GQ Drill," you will discover just how much money you can responsibly pay monthly towards the future home loan after you create your budget.

If you're not completely honest with yourself during this chapter, you may overextend financially and unknowingly sabotage your future. Don't ignore the data in your budget. Instead, listen to the actual numbers and readjust your strategy, as it will save you unnecessary financial and mental stress in the long run.

Before investing, I never had a budget. I scoffed at the notion. Like so many other Sailors, I knew that I would get paid religiously on the first and the fifteenth of each month like clockwork. I had an estimate of what I would receive, but I never bothered to calculate precisely. The arrogance of me to think my finances didn't deserve my time.

"God will never give you more than you can handle... this includes money too!" If you can't properly manage your current earnings, you won't manage a larger sum either. You must change your bad money habits if you are ever going to be financially successful. Up and down the chain of command, people struggle financially because they never successfully learned to manage their funds or control their spending. I've seen both Officers and Enlisted barely staying afloat as they lived paycheck to paycheck and beyond their means.

I knew I wanted to grow financially, so I sought advice from the Command Financial Specialist (CFS). Each command has a CFS representative. Although this is a collateral duty, to be selected as the CFS, the Sailor must undergo financial training and meet other criteria and be selected by the Commanding Officer. Most importantly, the CFS operates IAW the Privacy Act of 1974, in case you're worried about the privacy of your financial situation.

In short, I collected my shortlist of bills, and the Chief and I created a budget and a short-term plan together. Initially, the template was intimidating. It was built in PowerPoint and contained explosive sound effects, letters, and numbers flying across the screen – okay, not exactly, but it was a lot going on. I knew that If the budget process were too daunting, I wouldn't have followed through with it.

The budget we ultimately created was simple. Three columns were sufficient, as I didn't possess a lot of bills, and they were labeled as such; Section A represented income, Section B represented Expenses, and Section C was the remaining cash. Simple. Enough information to provide a brief overview of your financial standing.

As an example, amongst other areas, take a good look at the entertainment portion, which will be the most challenging part of your budget to adhere to. For clarity, use your bank statements from the past year to establish a baseline and review your past spending habits. By tallying individual categories, you can see trends and spending patterns. Cross-referencing your past spending habits with your new budget will provide valuable insight and offer a realistic approach to budgeting.

I wasn't in bad shape financially. However, one would argue not knowing where your money is going is just as bad, and now I agree.

Section C should have enough funds to cover your projected mortgage, utility insurance, and taxes in addition to your other bills. By law, lenders can't approve a mortgage that exceeds 35 percent of your monthly income. Therefore, it is important to pay down your debt to protect your debt-to-income ratio, as some lenders are known to enforce stricter numbers limiting borrowers to 28 percent.

Again, trust the numbers and only finance what you can comfortably afford to avoid becoming house poor. Visually, you can't see "house poor," as it is a person that has overextended themselves and is short of cash for discretionary purposes; remember Fonzo?

As a rule of thumb, while budgeting for monthly mortgage payments, note that for every $100k borrowed, you can estimate your monthly mortgage payments to be roughly $600. For example, a mortgage loan amount of $300k will be approximately $1,900 per month. The final price is ultimately contingent upon Private Mortgage Insurance (PMI), escrow, local state taxes, interest rates, Homeowners Association (HOA) dues, etc. Suppose you can successfully set aside the potential amount of your mortgage for at least three to six months. In that case, you have a higher success rate of not blowing your budget, ensuring funds are adequately allocated monthly for your future mortgage.

In this phase of your budget planning, do note that budgets are not concrete and can be adjusted to meet but should align with the overall goal of purchasing a home. If necessary, schedule an appointment with your Command Financial Specialist to start your budget planning process. Nowadays, there are a plethora of apps available to ease your budgeting process. Banking institutions also have budgeting tools built within accessible right from your phone. Review the two budgets; The current monthly budget for a renter and the projected monthly budget for a potential homeowner as an E5 with dependents are listed as examples.

RS2 Amiya Alston Monthly Budget

Monthly income for the month of: <u>December</u>

Item	Amount
Salary	3500
Spouse's salary	1500
Other	
Total	5000

Monthly expenses for the month of: <u>December</u>

Item	Amount
Rent	1500
Car loan	150
Car insurance	30
Renters insurance	15
Life insurance	35
Childcare	0
Saving	150
Gas/electricity	150
Telephone	80
Cable	30
Internet	50
Food	250
Healthcare	0
Entertainment	190
Gifts	100
Clothing	150
Other	
Total	**2880**

Income vs. Expenses

Item	Amount
Monthly income	5000
Monthly expenses	2880
Difference	2120

Sample Budget

RS2 Amiya Alston Future Monthly Budget

Monthly income for the month of: December

Item	Amount
Salary	3500
Spouse's salary	1500
Rental Income	500
Total	5500

Monthly expenses for the month of: December

Item	Amount
Mortgage	1000
Car loan	150
Car insurance	30
Home Owners Insurance	60
Life insurance	35
Taxes/Escrow	100
Saving	150
Gas/electricity	150
Telephone	80
Cable	30
Internet	50
Food	250
Healthcare	0
Entertainment	100
Gifts	50
Clothing	100
Other	
Total	2335

Income vs. Expenses

Item	Amount
Monthly income	5500
Monthly expenses	2335
Difference	3165

Sample Monthly Budget

Chapter Six

Choosing the Best Mortgage Loan For Your Situation

Home buying, particularly for real estate investment purposes, is not a one-size-fits-all. There are no bad mortgages, only mortgages that are more advantageous for you as a Service Member. Within this chapter, you will learn about the various types of mortgage loans and the pros and cons of each loan. There are several paths to obtain financing types of mortgage loans; Hard-Money, Investment / Commercial Property, Government-Insured, Jumbo, Conventional, Fixed-rate, FHA 2203k Rehab, Seller Financing, and Adjustable-rate mortgages. These loan options possess varying terms and conditions from one to the next, which doesn't make them bad loans. There may be a loan with terms that don't suit you and allow you to maximize your position, ultimately hindering your growth financially, but again the loans themselves are not bad.

Conventional Mortgage loans are loans that are not guaranteed or insured by a government entity, particularly the Federal Housing Administration (FHA), United States Department of Agriculture (USDA) Rural Housing Service, or the Department of Veteran Affairs (VA). The two types of conventional mortgage loans are conforming and non-conforming.

Conforming loans fall within Fannie Mae's or Freddie Mac's maximum limits; these government agencies back most U.S. mortgages. Within the continental U.S., the 2020 maximum conforming loan limit for one-unit properties is $510,400. Whereas loans that don't meet these guidelines and exceed $510,400 are considered non-conforming loans known as Jumbo mortgage loans. Without applying 20 percent as a down payment, your lender may require you to pay for private mortgage insurance (PMI). Your lender can remove PMI after paying down a portion of the principal and accruing 20 percent equity. PMI protects lenders in case the homeowner defaults on the home loan. It would behoove you to avoid PMI as it is costly over time. PMI can cost between $30 to $85 per month for every $100k financed or 0.50 and 1 percent of the mortgage annually. If you cannot afford the 20% down payment, be sure to factor PMI into your budget as a future expense.

After the housing crisis of 2008, Fixed-Rate Mortgages became ever more so popular. Fixed-rate mortgages maintain the same interest rate over the life of the loan. This fixed rate allows you to budget and makes long-term plans due to its consistency. This loan is for long-term investing as the loan terms for fixed-rate mortgages range from 15 to 30 years and require a more extended period to build up equity as you will pay more in interest over the life of the loan.

The housing crisis of 2008 changed real estate drastically. As a result, Adjustable Rate Mortgages (ARMs) financed homes have a bad reputation as most homes foreclosed during this time were via an ARM.

ARMs did lack stability in comparison to fixed mortgages, as the rates fluctuate based on market conditions. However, the market condition alone didn't solely cause the housing crisis, as fraudulent or inflated mortgage applications paired with lack of preparation for the swings in market shifts are also significant factors contributing to the crash. Since 2008, ARMs have been repackaged and have returned and now have stricter government regulating.

Post housing crises, a popular ARM option is the 5/1. The 5/1 option provides you with a low fixed interest rate of 3.75% for five years with a down payment as low as 5%. These changes offer a reprieve from the instability of older ARMs.

As mentioned earlier, Jumbo mortgages are conventional loans with non-conforming loan limits and exceed the federally backed home loan limit of $510,400. As of December 2020, the average home cost in San Francisco is $1.4M. Therefore, the use of jumbo loans in San Francisco is highly expected due to its relatively high-cost location. In addition to the required high credit score of 700 or higher, you must possess assets in the amount of ten percent of the loan in cash or other assets and cannot exceed a debt-to-income ratio of 45 percent. Additionally, a substantial amount of documentation may be required.

Investment loans are used when a single-family, townhome, condo, or multi-unit property has been purchased to earn a return on the investment, either through rental income, future resale, or both. The rates are typically higher than mortgages used for a primary residence and start at 5.25 percent if you have good credit. The loan may require more than 25 percent down payment depending on the unit as lenders consider investment and rental properties riskier. The loan duration is usually shorter than 30-year conventional mortgages and may require you to have a reserve of cash.

The U.S. Department of Agriculture (USDA loans), Federal Housing Administration (FHA loans), and the U.S. Department of Veterans Affairs (VA loans) are the type of Mortgages that are considered government-backed mortgages.

USDA loans help moderate- to low-income borrowers buy homes in rural areas. In addition, some USDA loans do not require a down payment for eligible borrowers with low incomes.

FHA loans make homeownership possible for borrowers who can't afford a large down payment required by other loan types or possess good credit. Borrowers need a minimum credit score of 580 to receive FHA's maximum 3.5 percent financing. However, a credit score of 500 and 579 is acceptable with at least 10 percent down. In addition, FHA loans require two mortgage insurance premiums: one is paid upfront, and the other is paid annually for the life of the loan if you put less than 10 percent down. This can increase the overall cost of your mortgage, which again should be factored into your budget.

VA loans, the crowd favorite amongst Veterans, provide flexible, low-interest mortgages for members of the U.S. military (active duty and Veterans) and their qualifying family members. On Tuesday, 25 June, H.R. 299, the Blue Water Navy Vietnam Veterans Act of 2019 was signed into law. This bill allows the Department of Veterans Affairs to back loans that exceed the standard conforming loan limit.

VA loans do not require a mandatory down payment or PMI, and closing costs are generally capped and may be paid by the seller. With specific stipulations, VA loans can be used more than once. A funding fee is charged on VA loans as a percentage of the loan amount to help offset the program's cost. The Department of Veteran Affairs can roll this fee and other closing costs into most VA loans or pay upfront at closing. If you are retired, a surviving spouse, and have a disability rating of ten percent or higher; your funding fees are waived. Funding fees are on average 3.3 percent. Funding The guaranteed government-backed VA home loan empowers lenders to provide you with more favorable terms. For example, there are no penalties for early pay-offs, mortgage assistance if you should run into financial trouble having difficulty making payments.

You should also know that aggressive sellers eager for a quick closing may avoid VA-backed financing as VA appraisals can be slow to process. A market advantageous to the seller is known as a sellers' market. In the wake of a sellers' market, multiple offers from other buyers are possible due to the demand for limited inventory. Depending on the seller's eagerness, may opt for different types of financing, i.e., conventional or cash.

Initially, I chose to opt out of using my VA loan to purchase my first investment property. Thinking long term, I knew I would invest more money into my "forever" home than I would be willing to do for an investment property and would prefer the maximum benefit of my no down payment VA loan not to be tied up. However, opting to use a conventional loan would require twenty percent down for a total of $80k for this particular investment property. The lack of down payment will keep you from obtaining a home. Fortunately, you and I are part of a unique group that entitles us to the VA loan. It is a powerful tool. Do note; the no money down factor does not absolve you from closing close, escrow, taxes, and other fees.

I used my benefits of the no money down appealing VA loan to get me in the house and then refinanced out of the program into a conventional loan with lower rates. This move allowed me to regain control of my VA loan for future use.

VA guidelines state that the property must be your primary residence for at least one year. It is prohibited to buy a home backed by VA for the sole purpose of using it outright as an investment property. Therefore, multi-family dwellings, i.e., duplex, triplex, quadruplex (VA prohibits financing on five or more units), make better initial investments. Opting to choose a multi-family unit provides you with a primary residence and an investment unit immediately instead of waiting until your transfer to your next duty station or waiting one full year (whichever comes first). You will receive immediate, predictable cash flow while living in the home, appreciates, provides equity buildup, you can leverage it, it's tax-deductible, it has a lower tax rate, and gains are deferrable. However, if you should find a great deal on a single-family home and have less than one year remaining at your current duty station – think long and hard before passing on the opportunity! Some single-family residences may net you more than a multi-family home. Remember, it's a numbers game, and if the numbers are favorable, do consider.

By law, the home financed by VA must be your primary residence for one year, or you risk voiding the terms and conditions and ultimately lose your benefits. PCS'ing due to military orders is one of the few times when you can move and rent the home, having had it for less than one year.

As stated earlier, there are no bad loans. Outlined below are some characteristics associated with the various types of loans for comparison.

Conventional Mortgages

Pros

•It can be used for a primary home or an investment property

•Potentially pay as little as 3% on Government-backed loans like Fannie Mae or Freddie Mac

•Lenders may cancel PMI once you've gained enough equity

Cons

•Credit score must be 620 or higher

•A debt-to-Income ratio of 45 to 50 percent

•Potentially pay PMI if the down payment is less than 20% of the sale price.

•Must provide proof to verify income, down payment assets, and employments via an absorbent amount of documentation.

Jumbo Mortgages

Pros

•Access to larger funding for costlier homes

•Interest rates are competitive with traditional conventional rates

Cons

•Down payments of at least 20 percent are required

•FICO scores are required to be 700 and higher

•A debt-to-income ratio above 45 disqualifies the borrower

•Must possess significant assets, ten percent of the loan in cash or other assets.

Government Insured Mortgages (FHA, VA, USDA)

Pros

•Credit Req's may be eased

•Large down payments aren't mandatory

•Programs help you finance a home loan when you can't qualify for conventional loans.

•Available for multiple uses and first-time home buyers.

Cons

•PMI is mandatory for the life of loans (except VA); however, after several years of on-time payments, The lender can remove it at the discretion of your lender.

•Providing documentation for proof of eligibility can be daunting

•Self-Sufficiency Test for Multi-Family

Fixed-Rate Mortgages

Pros

•Both Principal and Interest payments won't change throughout the life of the loan, which makes budgeting more straightforward and more precise.

Cons

•Due to a long-term fixed rate, you'll pay more interest

•Longer to acquire equity in the home

•Interest rates are higher when compared to ARMS

Adjustable Rate Mortgages (ARMs)

Pros

•Expect to save money due to low-interest rates

Cons

•Due to market fluctuations, payments could "balloon" & rise, causing you to default on your loan.

•If the housing market should take a dip, it may affect your property value – making it a challenge to sell your home loan before the loan reset.

Although I wrote this book with the premise of motivating Service Members to invest in real estate, you may not be in a financial position to do so. Look beyond federal programs, as your state may provide incentive programs' locally as well. For example; Under the MPAP Program, Washington D.C. offers its residence interest–free loans and closing cost assistance to qualified applicants to purchase single-family homes, condominiums, or cooperative units. Albeit, there are prerequisites and qualifying factors. As you transfer from duty station to duty station, you should research local housing incentive policies to see if you are eligible.

Chapter Seven

Obtain Certificate of Eligibility (COE)

If you choose to utilize your VA-backed home loan, the first step in the approval process is to obtain your Certificate of Eligibility (COE). This document will inform your lender that you qualify for a VA home loan.

Your duty status; Active Duty, Veteran, Reserve, etc., will determine how you obtain your COE. Active Duty Service Members are required to submit a statement of service signed by your Commanding Officer or Admin Officer. The statement of service must contain the following;

- Full Name
- Social Security Number
- Date of Birth
- Active Duty Service Date
- Duration of lost time (Break in Service if any)
- Name of Command/Duty Station Providing the Information

Retirees, Veterans, and members of the Reserves are only required to submit their DD 214. There are several methods to apply and obtain the COE. Eligible members can apply online via https://www.ebenefits.va.gov/ebenefits/about/feature?feature=cert-of-eligibility-home-loan (Requires Log-In). Qualified members may also apply by mail after completing the Request for a Certificate of Eligibility (VA Form 26-1880) and returning it to your regional office. Please review the site to obtain the most up-to-date form and address as information changes regularly.

Chapter Eight

Getting Lender Approved

Once you have verified your credit score is within approval range and aligns with the type of mortgage you will utilize to purchase a home, it's now the time to work to be pre-approved and lock in a great rate.

Finding a reputable mortgage lender is an integral part of finding a great price on a home. A mortgage lender is a financial institution that underwrites the home loan. There are so many companies to choose from, which may make the selection a daunting task. Odds are you may bank with the same institution that covers your insurance as well – which is fine. However, don't stress this right now, as loans are sometimes sold to other mortgage companies shortly after closing. Focus on competitive rates, customer service, fees, and approval criteria instead. If you have yet to select a lender and would like to shop around, consider working with an experienced mortgage broker experienced with the type of loan; VA, FHA, etc., you choose to streamline the process of shopping around for the best deal. Larger lenders have rigid approval criteria. At the same time, borrowers must meet all requirements. Smaller lenders will typically work with you and help assist you with rectifying any issues.

After you have made your selection, obtaining a pre-approval letter will be the next phase. This pre-approval letter is the result of an evaluation of your finances. Therefore, you must provide accurate data. The information you provide is an official offer by a lender but not a guarantee, based on your credit debt, income, and other assets.

At this phase of the home-buying process, the buyer should be serious as the letter only lasts for 90 days. The pre-approval letter also conveys to the realtor you are serious about moving forward. Documents necessary to initiate the pre-approval letter will differ from lender to lender. Personal documentation includes typically but is not limited to; bank statements, W-2's, prior-year tax records, pay statements, and TSP/401K documentation.

The home buying process does not always run from A to Z, as each scenario may slightly differ from one deal to the next. If you have already located a property, you may be ready to take further action to secure or lock in your mortgage rate utilizing a rate lock. A rate lock is essentially a freeze of the interest rate on the mortgage loan for a short period. Rates received before receiving a rate lock are only estimates and are not guaranteed. Although rates fluctuate, you could potentially save money by locking in your rate if the rates should rise.

VA loans don't require down payments should you select this rate. However, earnest fees may be required. Earnest money informs all parties that you are a serious buyer. Earnest money is negotiable but typically 1 to 3 percent of the total sale price and is held in an escrow account until the deal is complete. Earnest money protects the seller in the instance a buyer backs out of the agreement. To ensure your earnest money isn't forfeited, do not move forward until you are sure. Contingencies are defined as future events or circumstances which are possible but cannot be predicted with certainty. Realtors can write these clauses into the contract to protect the buyer. Ensure contingencies for financing, inspections, VA appraisals are entered into the contract. The purchase and sales agreement should contain a "VA Option

Clause." This clause will offer you an "escape" from the contract without a penalty in the instance you cannot obtain a VA loan. If the issues mentioned arise, the buyer may have to forfeit all funds if you decide to back out of the deal without these contingencies. If all goes smoothly, the earnest money is applied to the buyer's down payment cost.

Earnest money is not to be confused with cash for a down payment. A down payment is a set amount of money the buyer must produce before the lender approves the loan. Depending on the loan, the amount could range from 3 to 5 percent for FHA loans and 20 percent for conventional loans. In Chapter 5, paragraph four, I briefly spoke on the mail option to dispute in hopes of removing the late record from the report. Again, life happens. Thankfully, I wrote a letter of explanation (LOE) to the lender detailing what happened. The underwriter accepted the letter and processed the loan with no issues, as I could prove it was a one-time incident instead of reoccurring.

First, the housing bubble of 2008, now COVID19, has changed the landscape of real estate. Lenders' requirements are even more rigid than before. Due to the pandemic, the Fed (Federal Reserve) lowered the interest rates. With many Americans out of work and unable to pay mortgages, lenders are losing money. Unable to evict or foreclose, the best play was to offer forbearance. A forbearance offers the loan holder a chance to pay the mortgage at a lower rate or pause payments until a later date. Current homeowners are "grandfathered." As the gatekeepers of homeownership, lenders are scrutinizing new loan applicants with new requirements to avoid further loss. One current condition was in the form of an essay, which outlines the borrower's intentions and plans to ensure they can repay the loan on time.

Each mortgage company will have a list of requirements associated with a unique timeline. One of those items required and should not be put off is homeowner's insurance. Before signing, it is best to ascertain the cost of insuring the potential property to ensure you will meet your budget guidelines.

Chapter Nine

Acquiring A Down Payment From TSP/BSB/4O1K

The Thrift Savings Plan (TSP) is a government-created 401K plan that allows you to save for retirement, specifically for military and government civilians. The initial rollout of the TSP for active duty service members was in fall 2001. I remember the introduction of TSP. TSP had been around for quite some time for government-employed civilians. The day it was announced, my CO, CDR Drake, was so excited! CDR Drake asked if I had plans to invest in the program. I was a young Sailor at that time and knew little about investing. I replied, Sir, I don't even know what that is. Holding his signature coffee cup, he looked at me and said, well, it doesn't matter because you're signing up for 11 percent, which at that point was the max.

Initially, not having immediate access to the 11 percent of my salary took some getting used to. However, it later turned out to be one of the best decisions I ever made. I was always fortunate enough to be surrounded by great leaders and financially savvy men and women who served and always took an interest in my financial well-being.

Years later, semi-armed with knowledge of investing in real estate, I came across many properties that would have been significant assets, but the down payment placed them out of reach. Then, one day, I discovered that you could utilize your TSP and borrow your funds for a home loan. The money allocated to my savings had accrued significantly and was more than enough for a down payment.

Why is this important? If you opt for a loan that requires a large down payment, or if you're using your VA Loan for a second time, you may be required to pay a down payment. If that happens, consider borrowing from your TSP to purchase a multi-family property for your investment property. The TSP loan works as such; you may only borrow from what you have contributed to the account, not to exceed your contributions. The TSP program host two types of loans; general purpose and residential. General-purpose loans may be used for any purpose and must be repaid on terms not to exceed five years. Additional eligibility requirements must be active duty and inactive pay status as repayment is allocated via payroll deductions: one outstanding general-purpose and residential loan at a time. You must not have repaid a loan of the same type within the past 60 days nor have a court order against your account. You must budget accordingly, and factor in TSP loan repayment amounts into your budget should you opt to use your TSP. Often, investment goals are deviated due to the inability to repay the loan and make regular monthly contributions. Given your circumstances and financial objectives, a TSP loan may or may not make sense.

The authorized loan amount cannot exceed $50,000 and is repaid at the interest rate for the G Fund, which is currently 0.875 percent at the time of publishing, in addition to a $50 processing fee.

Some other benefits this may have over other loans are the interest paid goes directly back to you and your TSP account and can be paid back up to a period not to exceed 15 years. However, it does have some setbacks as well. For example, if you were to retire or exit the military service before repaying the loan, you must either pay the loan in full or be subject to a heavy tax burden on the unpaid balance. In addition, if your TSP funds were in any fund other than the G Fund before the loan, the rate of return of your initial TSP investment may be lower due to the interest rate of the G Fund.

Why is this important? If you opt for a loan that requires a large down payment, or if you're using your VA Loan for a second time, you may be required to pay a hefty down payment. If that happens, after you've performed your due diligence, consider borrowing from your TSP or other 401K investment funds towards the purchase of a multi-family property, such as a duplex or larger for your investment property. This option worked for me as the duplex I purchased as an investment property generated monthly income, and the property has grown in value.

To reiterate, if you ask 100 different people, you'll get 100 different answers. Withdrawing funds from your TSP to invest may be frowned upon and is a controversial topic. However, investing of any kind has risks, and this was the best viable option for me at the time. Carefully conduct a risk assessment to estimate how much you can tolerate.

Myths surrounding withdrawing funds from 401K type investments are claims of limiting and sacrificing growth. Investing requires strategic planning. Withdrawing money for vacations or to purchase depreciating assets like furniture, motorcycles, cars, etc., is never a wise idea. Although a controversial opinion, a home is an asset that appreciates over time and will serve as an investment. Growth due to perceived loss of investments from borrowed earnings over time is another factor to consider.

The earliest "traditional" retirement age to begin withdrawing funds from your 401K without penalty is 55. If you are investing, you are likely to invest for the future aggressively while you are younger, and as time draws nearer, you throttle back due to the lack of time to make up for any significant losses. Repaying the loan while making contributions can be challenging, but doing so may lessen the loss.

Non-TSP 401K retirement plans have penalties for early withdrawals. Therefore, if you held a 401K before enlisting, it might be best to merge your TSP and previously held 401Ks to avoid penalties.

Chapter Ten

Locating a Realtor

It has been my experience that the business relationship is better than the business transaction. You may receive a great deal, but you haggled the hard-working business ally that was willing to go above and beyond for you, and now you've ruined that relationship for future deals. If you're new to real estate, you should research and find a knowledgeable realtor with a proven track record of success.

Locating a realtor requires research. Nothing compares to the good old word of mouth and solid reviews; if you have an agent in mind, request references and speak to them about their experience with the agent, you are considering.

My realtor, Derrick Fuqua, located in San Diego, California, is hands down one of the best realtors I have ever worked with. Years of expertise with military processes, coupled with his hard-charging work ethic and around-the-clock availability, in addition to his network of real estate professionals and willingness to mentor and guide you every step of the way, makes him the most sought-after agent.

I've since moved away from San Diego but will routinely run a property thousand miles away by him to get a second opinion. If your realtor isn't performing as Mr. Fuqua has for me over the past decade, then you may want to reconsider. Before signing an agreement with a realtor whose face is plastered on every billboard, included are noteworthy traits you should look for in a realtor.

Realtors are in the business of all things concerning your home. When you select a realtor, not only can you tap into their expertise, but you also gain access to their network of real estate professionals. For instance, upon PCS'ing, your realtor may act as your property manager. Look for a realtor that wears multiple hats, property managers, etc. Using their resources, you gain access to their pool of already established renters.

As laws vary by location, your local realtor will be your subject matter expert keeping you abreast of pertinent local rules and information. For entry new investors, you must lean on your realtor to steer you clear of bad long-term investments.

Like most government-regulated practices that require a license, Citizens can review the holder. It is best to interview your potential agent before signing a contract. Ask for references of recent clients they have represented. All licensed agents possess an NMLS ID via the Nationwide Mortgage Licensing System. Upon obtaining the agent's NMLS ID, visit www.nmlsconsumeraccess.org. Anyone can find information such as place of employment, company representative authorization, and regulatory actions.

Your agent may require you to agree, which is a common practice. The agreement will state that you will work exclusively with the agent for a specified time, usually six months. Agent fees vary widely, and your agent may charge you an upfront fee. Due diligence on your part is of the utmost importance. Your realtor will be there to guide you throughout the process, but it is imperative that you thoroughly understand what you are signing. This reason alone should reaffirm your reasoning to interview your potential real estate agent. Your agent will receive 3 to 6 percent or even higher commission for representing you -make them earn it. Typically three for your agent and another three for the seller's agent.

If you are located in the National Capital Region (Washington D.C., Maryland, or Virginia) contact Ruby Harley at email via rharley118@gmail.com or via phone at (301)266-1619. If you are stationed in San Diego, C.A., contact Derrick Fuqua via email at Derrick.Fuqua@gmail.com.

Chapter Eleven

Locating A Property

At this point, you should have learned by now that the sole purpose is to steer you towards investing using the buy and hold, all while obtaining adequate lodging for you and your family. The buy and hold method is a long-term real estate investment strategy where a home is purchased and holds on to it while collecting rental income. Let's focus on a multi-family investment property. The VA will finance a multifunctional property with up to four units with no money down. Acquiring a multi-family property allows you to live in one unit while collecting rent on the other units.

After hiring a realtor, your job is far from over. It may be easy to adopt the fire and forget mindset, but "an action passed is not an action complete". Who knows what you desire for your family better than you? Therefore, you must pilfer through listings after providing your list of desires to your realtor; school zones, zoning, future development, resale, potential rentability, etc. Your agent will compile an MLS listing based on the criteria you provided.

It is essential to know the class of property in the area you are currently stationed by; i.e., Class A, Class B, and Class C. Property classifications make it easier to communicate the quality and rating of a property quickly and aid in the factor of rentability. Each class of property will represent a different level of risk and return. The classifications are assigned to properties after considering multiple factors such as; the age of the property, location of the property, tenant income levels, growth prospects, appreciation, amenities, and rental income. Utilize the class types in your decision-making process to consider how the property will fit within your investment strategy. There are three classes; Class A, Class B, and Class C. Class A properties represent the highest quality properties as they are 15 years or younger, desired by high-income earning tenants, and come included with top amenities. Class B properties are typically older than Class A properties and possess well-maintained buildings and are seen as value-add investment opportunities because the properties can be upgraded to Class B+ or Class A by renovations and additional improvements. Class C properties are 20 years and older and located in less than desirable locations. Class C properties tend to require renovations, to bring a modern standard. These properties have the lowest rental rates. Based on this information, which class of property do you currently reside in?

I think it is safe to say that we would all opt for a Class A property if given a choice for our living arrangements. However, as an early military investor, opting for this property class may counter intent and purpose. My go-to rule has always been to keep my target audience or pool of potential tenants as wide as possible. There is a small pool of people that can afford to live in Class A properties. Class C properties are affordable but are less than desirable by locations and quality of a property. Class B properties are in excellent areas and may be considered turnkey and require less upfront work. For an investor who desires capital preservation, Class A may be the better investment. Investors looking for capital appreciation, then Class B and Class C may be better investments for your specific risk profile.

Your realtor should provide you with properties that meet your criteria and that reflect your long-term investment strategy. Your realtor should also know the type of investment property you're interested in, i.e., Class B multi-family property. Aside from the desire to have an excellent property, operating with the end goal in mind, the Return on Investment (ROI) is the most crucial factor for your rental property. The ROI is the measure of how much money you make over the life of holding the property. The goal is to make more than you initially put into the investment, i.e., the home. This again is why the VA home loan with no money down provides a considerable advantage for Service Members. Calculating your ROI can be a complicated process depending on how you acquire your home (cash or finance). A recent property financed as such; a purchase price of $85k using the no money down VA financing option at a modest 2.5 percent interest rate for 30 years with a closing cost at $3k will produce a mortgage payment of $335 per month. When calculating insurance, property tax, a vacancy rate of 5 percent yields an NOI of $930 with a cash flow of $593 per month. Fundamentals don't change; adhering to basic guidelines such as the 1 to 3% rule or the 50% rule can reveal desirable properties. The gross monthly income for the property used based on the criteria provided of $85k.

First Year Income and Expense

	Monthly	Annual
Income:	$1,250.00	$15,000.00
Mortgage Pay:	$335.85	$4,030.23
Vacancy (5%):	$62.50	$750.00
Property Tax:	$45.83	$550.00
Total Insurance:	$66.67	$800.00
HOA Fee:	$45.83	$550.00
Maintenance Cost:	$83.33	$1,000.00
Other Cost:	$16.67	$200.00
Cash Flow:	**$593.31**	**$7,119.77**
Net Operating Income (NOI):	$929.17	$11,150.00

Sample Personal Income and Expenses Report

Utilizing the 50% rule to "estimate" the NOI, one should estimate operating expenses to be 50 percent of the gross income, excluding mortgage cost. Remember, finding a suitable place to live in addition to positive cash flow is the goal. The breakdown of the property mentioned above using the 50% rule is as follows;

50% of the rental income of $1,250 per month = $625

12 months multiplied by $625 = $7,500

$3,000 closing cost plus the price of home =$85,000

$7,500 divided by the total cost $85,000 = 11%

By standard, this is a good buy. Typically on just the numbers alone, 6% is a good indicator of the financial potential. However, this property teeters at 11.3% and will increase as time passes and rent increases. In short, the property must generate enough income/cash flow to be considered a good investment for the long term, and in part, following the fundamental rules will help you reach this conclusion.

Do note, as there are many variables, this formula would assume you are using the VA no money down option, with 2.5% financing at 30 years. This is a soft analysis, and it is used early in the home shopping process to ascertain if you should investigate further. Playing with different numbers before will also help you speed up the process and steer you towards specific price ranges.

Although not currently required for VA financing, FHA financing requires multi-family homes to pass the self-sufficiency test. The self-sufficiency test is the total rent that you receive for the units must be equal to or greater than the mortgage payment.

Odds are your realtor will input your criteria into a database, and the system will automatically forward you a compiled list based on that criteria. Other online sites offer you a chance to search and learn what else may be available.

As previously mentioned, San Diego is rated as a top choice for thousands of service members because it has a lot to offer. In addition to service members, some civilians are vying to obtain a slice of California's rare land. Low inventory and high demand are vital components for a hot market. During my time in San Diego, I looked at countless multi-family units. Unfortunately, I was either out bided, and the location was less than desirable due to safety concerns, issues with VA appraisals, or other hurdles. After the tenth time, I grew tired, and to be honest, and I was ready to call it quits. Fortunately, that wasn't an option. One night while searching through the slim inventory of listings, I stumbled across a new construction multi-family property. In 2012 the purchase price was $408K – today, the property is worth $790K and rising. Located in University City (UC), the area was in a period of transition. I rented each three-bedroom unit for $2,200 per unit. After paying the insurance, mortgage, and on-call handyman, I opted out of property management due to an interpersonal relationship I established before PCSing. The property netted $2k per month.

In its heyday, UC was a crime-filled area. Military members lived in Chula Vista, Mission Valley, Mira Mesa, or other regions with better schools. School zones were not an immediate issue for me, as I did not have a school-aged child during this time. North Park, a neighborhood adjacent to UC, was at peak demand. A collective of hipsters, young professionals, and students primarily reside in the bustling upscale area. The location of the multi-family unit was a brisk walk away.

Location is key. It is not necessary to be in the best house on the best block in the best neighborhood. Emotions driven by ego are a must to avoid. Under the buy and hold investment strategy, always think long-term. You may wish to consider; What are the major plans for the neighborhood or city? Via the city website, you can obtain development plans for the area of interest. By virtue, I believe it is safe to say that most men and women serving in the military are adventurous. I encourage you to get out and explore your potential neighborhood. Explore the area in the early morning and late evenings on both weekdays and weekends. Visit the possible site on rainy days to view grading and flooding possibilities.

University City is near major highways, hospitals, and a significant public transportation depot. However, the community did experience a moment of being labeled a food desert. The only supermarket within miles temporarily closed its doors. This issue may be an area of concern if you rent to seniors in the future.

Throughout my time in California, I owned two cars. My home did not have cameras or an active alarm system. I deployed for long periods, and I also traveled out of the country on vacation for weeks at a time. My home nor my belongings were never damaged or burglarized. Some will advise you to purchase the cheaper property in a neighborhood prone to violence, but safety should be paramount, and spending more for a turnkey provides one less worry. No community is free from crime, but it's better to be safe than sorry. Granted, I was neighbors with the San Diego Police Department – I never worried at all.

No one goes in business to go broke or break even. In part, the multifaceted goal is to make money while building a real estate portfolio and leave a legacy for your loved ones to build. School zones, location, and crime are all essential factors and will affect rentability in the future, but never become emotionally attached to a property. Regardless of how lovely the property may be, it is essential to know that it is no different than a wrench or a hammer. It is a tool. Real estate is business, so the sooner you become emotionally sterile towards your property, the better off you will be to make sound business decisions. First-time homebuyers may find it challenging to forego their dream home and opt for a duplex or multi-family property. The multi-family property may be financially advantageous over the single-family home. However, it ultimately comes down to a numbers game. The multi-family property may also allow you the flexibility of potentially living rent-free, as the rent collected from your tenant may cover the entire mortgage. Furthermore, upon PCSing you will collect rental income from more than one unit. This home is not your forever home – so do not become attached as you will possibly PCS/rotate within three to five years.

Chapter Twelve

Make An Offer and Negotiate

If not already, this is where your agent has an opportunity to shine. Once you've found your dream investment property that meets the criteria provided to your realtor – you're considered a motivated buyer.

Before making an offer, your agent must do the homework. First, your agent will run comparisons to the home you have selected against the last three to five homes of similar stature sold within a one to three-mile radius with similar characteristics of the house on the market. Commonly referred to as "running comps" or comparable sales. Comps help determine if the home is overpriced or priced appropriately at market value. After reviewing comps', your agent will make recommendations as to the expert you chose. Finally, you and your agent will agree on a fair offer to submit. Ultimately, you have to live with the outcome, so be sure to iron things out before submitting an offer to the seller's agent. Listed within is an example of a comp.

Small Residential Income Property Appraisal Report   File #   77-7

FEATURE	SUBJECT	COMPARABLE SALE # 4	+(-) Adjustment	COMPARABLE SALE # 5	+(-) Adjustment	COMPARABLE SALE # 6	+(-) Adjustment
Address	San Diego, CA 92105	47th St San Diego, CA 92105		42nd St San Diego, CA 92105		Swift Ave San Diego, CA 92104	
Proximity to Subject		0.64 miles SE		0.32 miles SW		1.04 miles W	
Sale Price	$ 408,000	$ 429,999		$ 475,000		$ 485,000	
Sale Price/Gross Bldg. Area	$ 211.00 sq.ft.	$ 270.78 sq.ft.		$ 231.46 sq.ft.		$ 276.67 sq.ft.	
Gross Monthly Rent	$ 2,700	$ 2,850		$ 2,995		$ 3,245	
Gross Rent Multiplier	151.11	150.88		158.60		149.46	
Price per Unit	$ 204,000	$ 215,000		$ 158,333		$ 242,500	
Price per Room	$ 45,333	$ 53,750		$ 39,583		$ 60,625	
Price per Bedroom	$ 81,600	$ 107,500		$ 79,167		$ 80,833	
Rent Control	☐ Yes ☒ No	☐ Yes ☒ No		☐ Yes ☒ No		☐ Yes ☒ No	
Data Source(s)		MLS/TITLE CO.:DOM 56		MLS/TITLE CO.:DOM 139		MLS/TITLE CO.:DOM 15	
Verification Source(s)		mls#12-0035051		mls#12-0035051		DOC#12-522522	
VALUE ADJUSTMENTS	DESCRIPTION	DESCRIPTION	+(-) Adjustment	DESCRIPTION	+(-) Adjustment	DESCRIPTION	+(-) Adjustment
Sale or Financing Concessions		active listings		active listings		ArmLth CONVENTIONAL	
Date of Sale/Time		07/11/2012		07/11/2012		08/30/2012	
Location	AVG/TRAFFIC	AVERAGE	-10,000	AVERAGE	-10,000	AVERAGE	
Leasehold/Fee Simple	Fee Simple	Fee Simple		Fee Simple		Fee Simple	
Site	5,800 Sq.Ft.	6,250 sf	0	7,000 sf	0	7,000 sf	0
View	N;Res;	N;Res;		N;Res;		N;Res;	
Design (Style)	BUNGALOW	BUNGALOW		BUNGALOW		BUNGALOW	
Quality of Construction	AVERAGE	AVERAGE		AVERAGE		AVERAGE	
Actual Age	88	55	0	55	0	91	0
Condition	GOOD	GOOD		AVERAGE	+25,000	GOOD	
Gross Building Area	1,936.7	1,588	+14,000	2,052	-5,000	1,753	+7,000
Unit Breakdown	Total Bdrms Baths	Total Bdrms Baths		Total Bdrms Baths		Total Bdrms Baths	
Unit # 1	5 3 2	4 2 1	+8,000	4 2 1	+8,000	5 3 2	
Unit # 2	4 2 1	4 2 1		4 2 1		3 3 1	+3,000
Unit # 3				4 2 1	-35,000		
Unit # 4							
Basement Description	0	0sf		0sf		0sf	
Basement Finished Rooms	0	0		0		0	
Functional Utility	ADEQUATE	ADEQUATE		ADEQUATE		ADEQUATE	
Heating/Cooling	WALL/NONE	WALL/NONE		WALL/NONE		WALL/NONE	
Energy Efficient Items	NONE NOTED	NONE NOTED		NONE NOTED		NONE NOTED	
Parking On/Off Site	OPEN PARKING	OPEN PARKING		1 GARAGE	-10,000	1 GARAGE	-10,000
Porch/Patio/Deck	PORCH/PATIO	PORCH/PATIO		PORCH/PATIO		PORCH/PATIO	
FIREPLACES	0 FP	0 FP		0 FP		0 FP	
UPGRADES	GOOD	GOOD		AVERAGE	+25,000	GOOD	
POOL	NO POOL/SPA	NO POOL/SPA		NO POOL/SPA		NO POOL/SPA	
Net Adjustment (Total)		☒ + ☐ -	$ 12,000	☐ + ☒ -	$ -2,000	☐ + ☐ -	$ 0
Adjusted Sale Price of Comparables		Net Adj. 2.8 % Gross Adj. 7.4 %	$ 441,999	Net Adj. 0.4 % Gross Adj. 24.8 %	$ 473,000	Net Adj. 0 % Gross Adj. 4.1 %	$ 485,000
Adjusted Price Per Unit (Adj. SP Comp / # of Comp Units)		$ 221,000		$ 157,667		$ 242,500	
Adjusted Price Per Room (Adj. SP Comp / # of Comp Rooms)		$ 55,250		$ 39,417		$ 60,625	
Adjusted Price Per Bedrm (Adj. SP Comp / # of Comp Bedrooms)		$ 110,500		$ 78,833		$ 80,833	

Report the results of the research and analysis of the prior sale or transfer history of the subject property and comparable sales (report additional prior sales on page 3).

ITEM	SUBJECT	COMPARABLE SALE # 4	COMPARABLE SALE # 5	COMPARABLE SALE # 6
Date of Prior Sale/Transfer	06/04/2010			03/23/2012
Price of Prior Sale/Transfer	$212,000			$275,000
Data Source(s)	MLS/DATA QUICK	MLS/DATA QUICK	MLS/DATA QUICK	MLS/DATA QUICK
Effective Date of Data Source(s)	09/05/2012	09/05/2012	09/05/2012	09/05/2012

Analysis of prior sale or transfer history of the subject property and comparable sales   COMP 6 WAS PURCHASED OUT OF FORECLOSURE ON 03/23/2012 FOR $275,000 AND THEN REMODELED AND UPDATED. PRIOR TO THAT IT WAS FORECLOSED UPON ON 11/21/2011 FOR $535,417.

Analysis/Comments   COMP 4 IS A SMALLER TWO UNIT BUILDING WITH SIMILAR UPGRADES AND REMODELING. IT ADDS GREATER WEIGHT TO THE VALUE INDICATED. IT WAS LISTED ON 07/11/2012.
COMP 5 IS A SIMILAR SIZE THREE UNIT BUILDING WITH NO UPGRADES OR REMODELING. IT HAS A ONE CAR GARAGE AND ADDS GREATER WEIGHT TO THE VALUE INDICATED. IT WAS LISTED ON 07/11/2012.
COMP 6 IS A RECENT SALE INCLUDED DUE TO ITS SIMILAR REMODELING AND UPDATING. IT IS SMALLER WITH LESS BATHS AND A ONE CAR GARAGE.

THE BEDROOM ADJUSTMENTS WERE BASED ON $5,000 PER BEDROOM, $3,000 PER BATHS AND $40 PER SQUARE FOOT.

Sample Appraisal Report

After retiring, I worked as an Analyst in the Office of Under Secretary of Defense for Policy as a DoD Contractor. Enlisting in the military immediately after high school, the U.S. Navy was my first significant job, so negotiating salary isn't a way of life for military personnel. Before retiring, you're introduced via transitioning programs an overview on negotiating. My first offer was $30K less than what I made while on active duty. My second offer was equivalent to my active duty pay. It's all comes down to knowing the value. Yes, the appraisal is a safety net, but you should learn from your realtor the home's actual value before making an offer. One day, you too will hang up your uniform and bid your service farewell, and you may find yourself negotiating your salary, and it is imperative to know your worth.

Negotiating in real estate happens in a seller's or buyer's market. A buyers market is merely more people seeking to buy homes than people willing to sell their homes. A seller's market is defined as more people selling their homes than people willing to purchase homes. If appropriate, you may get away with offering ten percent less than the asking price in a buyer's market. An eager seller may negotiate to cover the closing costs. A seller's market, due to demand, may require that you pay above the asking price. If your offer is too lay, it may not be accepted or considered due to demand. The seller has the upper hand and, due to demand, may hold out for what they feel is a better deal. Work with a real estate professional and negotiate a purchase agreement comfortable for your budget to make negotiations minimal.

Chapter Thirteen

Home Inspection

You may recall my earlier mentioning of the 2008 Housing Crisis. During that time, the housing market was essentially at a standstill. The banks weren't lending, delaying the home buying process for buyers. As a result, a lot of hard-working Americans were affected by the crisis.

It took a while before the housing market recovered. Some areas experienced far worse than others. Pairing the Housing Crisis with Nevada's 2008 budget crisis, Las Vegas was hit hard economically. If you had the cash, it was a buyers' market.

I would drive to Las Vegas, Nevada, from San Diego, searching for the next great deal each weekend. The most impressive community possessed 12 standalone buildings with 48 doors and a $425K asking price. The local economy was in terrible shape, as houses were continually being foreclosed. The rental community took a hit as Las Vegas is an attraction/tourist town and depends primarily on the tourist dollar, which was practically non-existent as Americans cut back on spending.

I was ready for the long-term financing to cover down if future tenants didn't cover rent. I was eager but not too keen to forego a home inspection with a contingency clause on a property of this magnitude.

What is a home inspection? A home inspection serves to assure the potential buyer that the property has no significant defects, and if it does, the inspector shall report such findings. If conducted properly, a thorough home inspection will provide you with reliable information on your potential property ranging from the roof's condition, structure, foundation, plumbing, HVAC systems, crawlspaces, basements, insects, or rodents and much more.

For me, receiving a home inspection report is equivalent to receiving a gift on Christmas morning for a child. It places you a step closer to the home buying process. Investing has its share of highs and lows. This particular property had severely flawed, and the old pipes were destroyed and damaged by sprawling roots in all of the buildings. As a result, raw sewage flowed directly onto the ground under the units. It was a job that I didn't want to take on at the time.

After you receive information from a trusted home inspector, you must determine whether you will proceed with acquiring the property. Unfortunately, the home inspection contingency clause coupled with the home inspection findings essentially gave me an out as the seller was unwilling to negotiate the asking price or make the necessary repairs.

Although home inspections are not required, had I not spent the $300, I would have acquired a property that required thousands of dollars in repair cost alone. You may wish to choose to spend or save money elsewhere, but don't skimp out over a couple of hundred dollars. I highly recommend obtaining a home inspection to avoid future headaches.

The potential buyer can sue a home inspector if they are negligent in their reporting, should proof of inadequate inspecting arise later. Opt for a reputable licensed home inspector. Your seasoned realtor should assist in this area.

If you would like to learn as much as you can about the entire process, speak with your home inspector and inquire about accompanying and being present during the inspection. Your inspector can point out obvious things along the way. Avoid being a distraction so your inspector can focus entirely on finding as much as possible. My first home inspector was terrific, and he took the time to walk me through the entire process.

Now would be a great time to have the inspector look for things that may cause you to fail the Section 8 inspection. Section 8 is a subsidy for low-income citizens for payment of rental housing. Home specifications and requirements vary by state.

Visit the Housing and Urban Development site at HUD.gov https://www.hud.gov/sites/documents/52580.PDF to obtain a comprehensive list of essentials. Working with your inspector as part of your strategy can identify items that would disqualify you from renting to Section 8 tenants in the future.

Chapter Fourteen

Veteran Affairs Appraisals

If you should opt to use your VA Loan, the property must undergo the appraisal process. A home inspection is often mistaken for a VA Appraisal. However, a home inspection is much more thorough. The main goal of the VA Appraisal is to assess the value and condition of the property by an independent appraiser.

VA appraisals are more brutal to pass and add at least three weeks to the home buying process, making an eager seller uncomfortable when the buyer is aware of the VA process. Additionally, if the home appraises for far less than the asking price, The Department of Veterans Affairs cannot issue a VA loan for more than the appraisal value. The buyer must make up the difference. For example, a home listed for an asking price of $300K can get a VA offer with total financing if it appraises at $300K or more. If the appraiser states the home listed at $300K appraises and is worth $200K, then the VA will finance $200K, and the buyer must provide the remaining $100K.

While in San Diego, in the beautiful town of Lemon Grove, there was a beautiful triplex with an asking price of $575,000. The seller owned it outright, but he broke what I believe to be the number one rule in real estate investing. "Do not become emotionally attached to the property." Doing so hinders sound judgment and makes for bad business decision-making.   The seller placed a lot of sweat equity into the property.   It was visible with the level of attention to detail he put into the property.

However, no matter what you've done to a property, the current market rate establishes the worth.   I was eager to add this already set with the tenant's triplex to my portfolio.   We attempted to negotiate with the seller, but old millionaires are stubborn!   We continued with the attempt to purchase and hopefully use the appraisal to solidify our bargaining measures.
My realtor Derrick Fuqua warned the seller that it wouldn't appraise, and it one hundred percent did NOT!   The seller was not willing to budge on the asking price, so the deal eventually fizzled flat.

Months later, I would occasionally drive by the property that got away.   It sat there on the market for months as it should.   I welcome appraisals.   A subject matter expert ensuring that the deal is sound protects the big guys with deeper pockets and protects you and me as veterans.

Aside from not possessing the asking price value, other items of interest that cause VA appraisals to fail are; termite and pest issues, broken windows, roof requiring significant repairs, faulty wiring & electrical systems, and insufficient heating.

Chapter Fifteen

Closing On Your Home

The closing represents the final lap on your journey to wealth building through homeownership. Our closing date will be the day you legally become a homeowner. First, you and the seller agree upon the date. Then, the lender chooses a title company, an attorney, or one of their representatives to conduct the closing. This person will coordinate the date/time, and a Closing attorney will transfer the property. If you have any questions during the process that the lender can't answer to your satisfaction, please get in touch with VA at your Regional Loan Center by calling 1-877-827-3702 with hours of operation from 8 am to 6 pm.

At your closing, you will have the option to buy "Mortgage points" or "buy down the rate." One point is estimated to cost 1% of the mortgage, i.e., $1,000 for every $100,000 financed. These fees are paid directly to the lender at closing in exchange for reduced interest rates. This tactic will lower your monthly mortgage payments. This option is an excellent tool for a borrower with not-so-good credit. Do note that each lender has its price structure.

As of 2019, the IRS also allows you to deduct the total amount of your points in the year you pay for them as a tax incentive. Closing costs are two to four percent of the purchase price. If anything should arise during the closing process, you will have to write a Letter of Explanation (LOE) outlining details of the item in question.

During your closing process, the lender chooses a title company, an attorney, or one of their representatives to conduct the closing. This person will coordinate the date/time, and the property will transfer. If you have any questions during the process that the lender can't answer to your satisfaction, please get in touch with VA at 1-877-827-3702.

Fees associated with closing costs will vary, but it is essential to factor in this cost to avoid last-minute surprises. In the instance the seller does not pay your closing cost, if applicable as the buyer, you are responsible for the following fee's;

Lender Fees
- Origination
- Application
- Appraisal
- Flood Certification
- Discount Points

Escrow Charges
- Homeowners insurance
- Escrows
- Property Tax Escrows

Title & Closing Fees
- Title Exam / Closing Fee
- Title Insurance Premiums
- Recording Fees
- Prorated Property Taxes
- Prorated HOA Dues

Chapter Sixteen

The Active Duty Entrepreneurs Guide to Readying Your Home for Tenants

COMING SOON

The Active Duty Entrepreneurs Guide to Readying Your Home for Tenants

After you've completed this book, I urge you to purchase part two of this book, "The Active Duty Entrepreneurs Guide to Readying Your Home for Tenants," for further in-depth guidance. Utilizing these books in tandem will further prepare you for your role as a Military Real Estate Investor.

Thank you for your purchase, but most importantly, I wish you nothing but success in your military career and endeavors as a Military Real Estate Investor.

www.ingramcontent.com/pod-product-compliance
Lightning Source LLC
La Vergne TN
LVHW051815080426
835513LV00017B/1962